a little book of ACE

by clara dehlin

this book belongs to

Natasha Pilipuf

to all my aspec pals out there:

I see you, you matter, and you are loved!

best wishes,
clara

this book is dedicated to

you.

A quick disclaimer before we get started:

I have done my best to write this book in an inclusive and thoughtful way. However, I am sure that I did not get everything perfect. Everyone's personal experiences and identities are so different and unique to themselves. This book is meant to inform about different concepts surrounding asexuality in an easily digestible format. Because of the overlap between communities, it also includes some information about aromanticism as well.

table of contents

part one: education
(pg. 6)

part two: quotes
(pg. 47)

part three: reflection
(pg. 60)

part four: identities index
(pg. 70)

part five: resources
(pg. 77)

part one: education

some terms to know

asexual (ace)- a sexual orientation defined by a lack of sexual attraction

allosexual- someone who feels sexual attraction towards others

aromantic (aro)- a romantic orientation defined by a lack of romantic attraction

alloromantic- someone who feels romantic attraction towards others

sexual attraction- when a person desires sexual contact with or shows sexual interest in someone else

romantic attraction- when a person desires romantic contact or interaction with someone else

platonic attraction- the desire for a platonic relationship or friendship with someone

libido- a person's overall sexual drive or desire for sexual activity

amatonormativity- the widespread assumption that everyone should be seeking and desiring an exclusive, romantic, long-term relationship, and the pressure- especially on aspec folks- this assumption creates

queerplatonic/quasiplatonic relationship (qpr)- a type of relationship that goes beyond what is the subjective cultural norm for a friendship. they may not be sexual or romantic, but signify a more intense level of commitment, companionship, and/or love than a platonic friendship

aspec- the asexual or aromantic spectrum

split attraction model (sam)- a model of attraction representing the idea that romantic and sexual attraction are two different concepts that may at times even be in opposition to one another

squish- the word for a platonic crush, used frequently in aspec communities

so what is attraction, anyway?

that's a really great question!

there are all types of things that can draw us towards another person, and not all of them involve the stereotypical ideas of attraction.

Benefits O. Center
855-322-2363

let's say you move to a new school and meet a really cool guy named jasper. you think he's super rad and love the way he does his hair and the clothes he wears. overall, you really admire his style and how he looks.

jasper

this is called *aesthetic attraction*

and maybe your best friend rory is the perfect person to spend time with when you're wanting to connect with someone. they have such an engaging personality and you love asking them about how they see things. you feel safe enough to tell them anything.

rory

this is called *emotional attraction*

maybe there's someone that you love to hug and cuddle with during movies, even though you may not feel romantically about them.

this is called *sensual attraction*

and how about the kid next door that you love to talk about outer space with? you both could have a conversation for hours about the physics of the planets in our solar system.

this is called *intellectual attraction*

what does that all mean?

it means that there are a lot of ways to feel drawn to people, and a lot of them are *platonic.* asexual or aromantic people may not feel sexual or romantic attraction towards anyone, but that doesn't mean that they aren't able to feel attracted to other people in different ways.

✳✳✳

there is a common misconception that asexual or aromantic people do not want to be in relationships, but that is not always the case! in a survey of over 400 aspec individuals, 65% said they wanted a partnered relationship in the future in some form.

it just might look a bit different than what society has taught you is the "norm".

what kinds of attraction do I experience?

- ☐ sexual
- ☐ romantic
- ☐ platonic
- ☐ aesthetic
- ☐ emotional
- ☐ sensual
- ☐ intellectual
- ☐ _____
- ☐ _____

the analogy of cake
in a comparison to sex

cake is pretty yummy. most people think so, at least. but imagine if everyone around you was *obsessed* with cake.

your friends love to tell you about the last cake they had and who they had it with.

at work, people love to make jokes about cake.

your parents are concerned that you maybe haven't tried cake yet.

movies and books usually have at least one cake scene three-fourths through.

but for you, cake might not really cross your mind all that often.
or maybe you like the idea of cake, but when you actually try it, it's not for you.
or maybe you just straight up hate cake. and that's okay too!

cake can be great, sure, but what's with all the hype about it? doesn't really make a whole lot of sense.

but you thinking that way makes people very uncomfortable.

"maybe you just haven't tried the right kind of cake"

↓

"did you ever have some cake related trauma when you were a child?"

↓

"are you sure you don't want cake? here, try it just in case!"

"no thank you, darlene!"

because just like you know when you want cake, you know when you don't.

there doesn't need to be a lengthy experimental process to figure that out.

what does it mean to be...

sex repulsed: "cake is gross!"

sex averse: "I don't like cake, but I can see why other people like cake."

sex indifferent: "I don't have any strong feelings about cake."

sex favorable: "I love cake!"

people on the ace spectrum can feel all different ways about sex.

turtles in a pond

an aspec analogy

the process of figuring out if you are ace or aro can be so much more difficult than other sexualities, because it's like trying to find the absence of something.

let's say you have a pond and you want to know if there are any turtles or fish in your pond.

maybe you spot a turtle and you're like "cool! my pond has turtles!"

maybe you spot a fish and you're like "awesome! my pond has fish!"

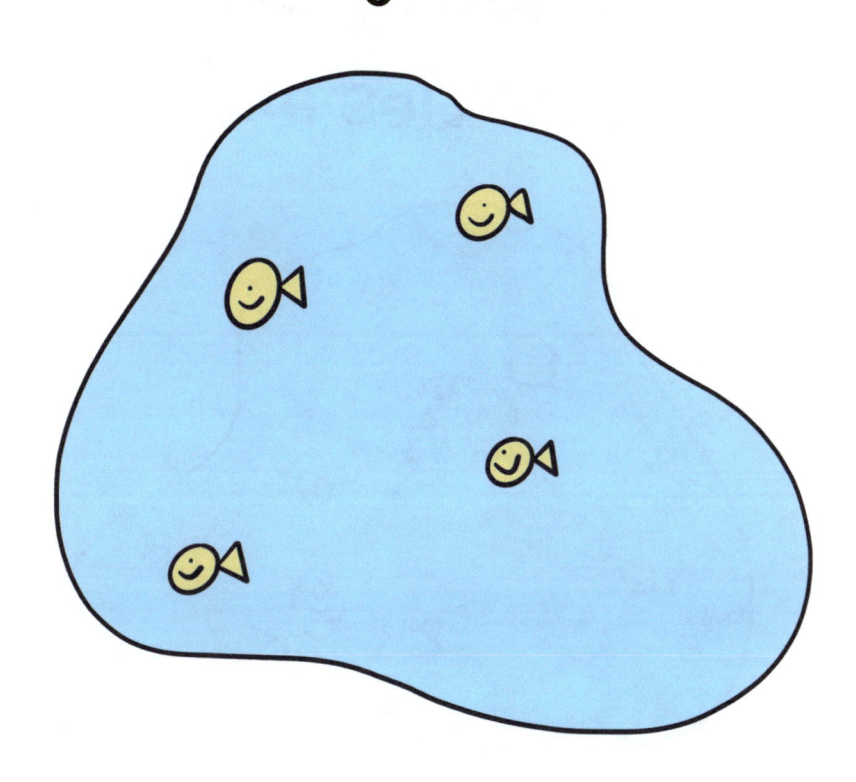

and maybe you find turtles *and* fish, and you're stoked to know that your pond has both turtles and fish.

but maybe you're looking really hard and you don't really see any turtles. maybe there aren't any turtles in your pond at all. but what if you just really suck at looking for turtles? what if that rock over there is actually a turtle and you're just not looking hard enough?

maybe you have to do something special for the turtles to come out. maybe there's only one turtle and it's really small and hiding. maybe all of those rocks are turtles but they just really look like rocks.

or maybe, there are just no damn turtles anywhere.

but hey! your pond is looking just lovely whether it has turtles or no turtles.

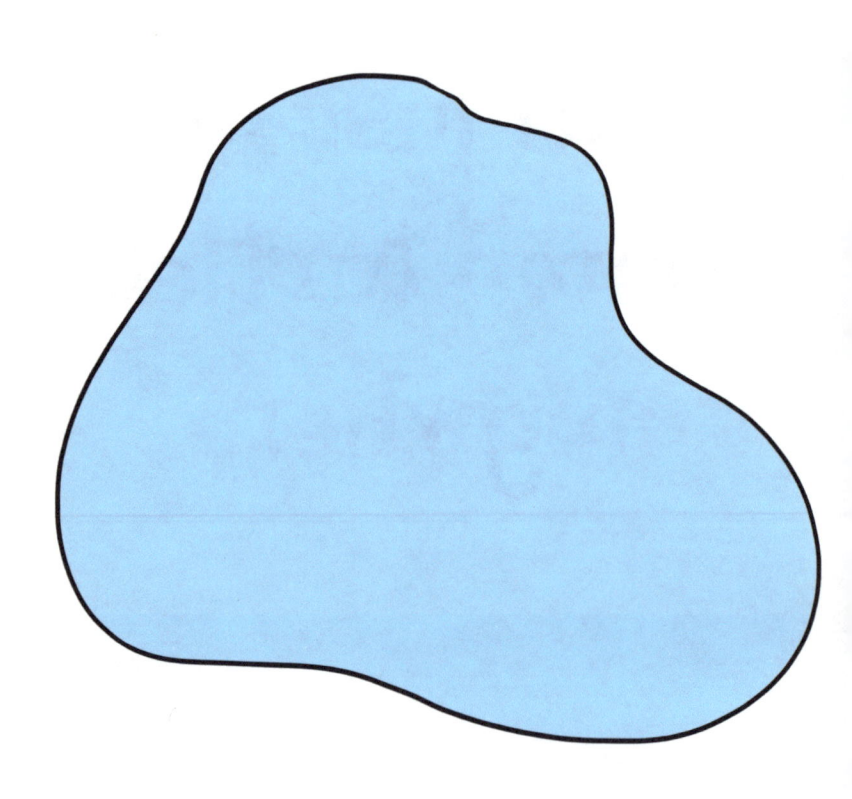

so here's the thing.

you don't have to be *entirely sure.*
you don't have to search *every centimeter* of your pond before you can decide that there are probably no turtles in it.
if you want to take the aro or ace label because you think it fits, go for it.
and if you do find your turtles, you can rename the pond. that's okay.

and if people say: "oh no!!! what disaster happened to your pond that made all the turtles go away???"

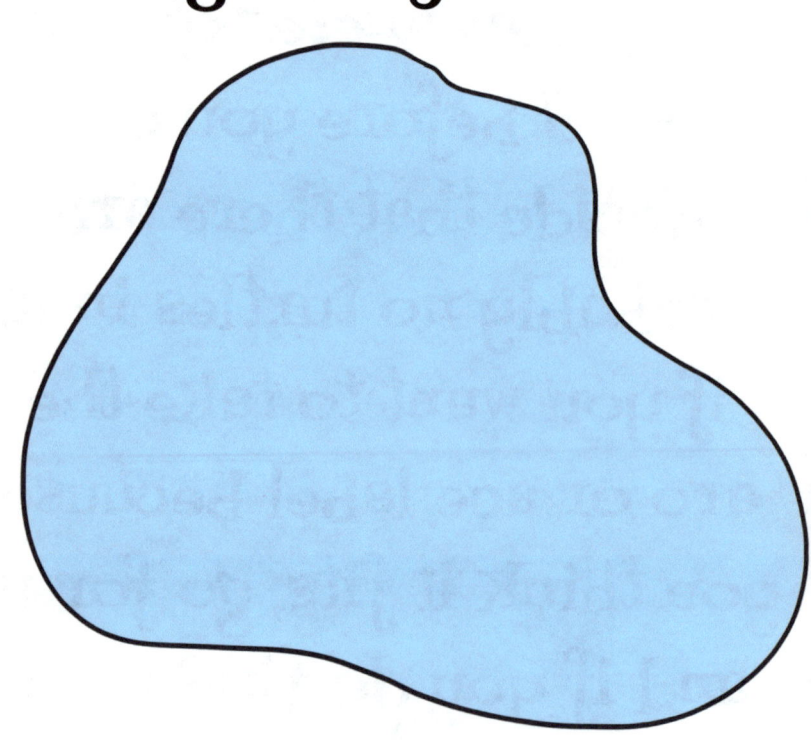

"hey! my pond is doing just fine without turtles. and if someone tried to add turtles to my pond, that could affect the whole ecosystem of the water and really mess things up. so let's just all calm down about turtles, okay?"

what does your pond look like?
draw it below

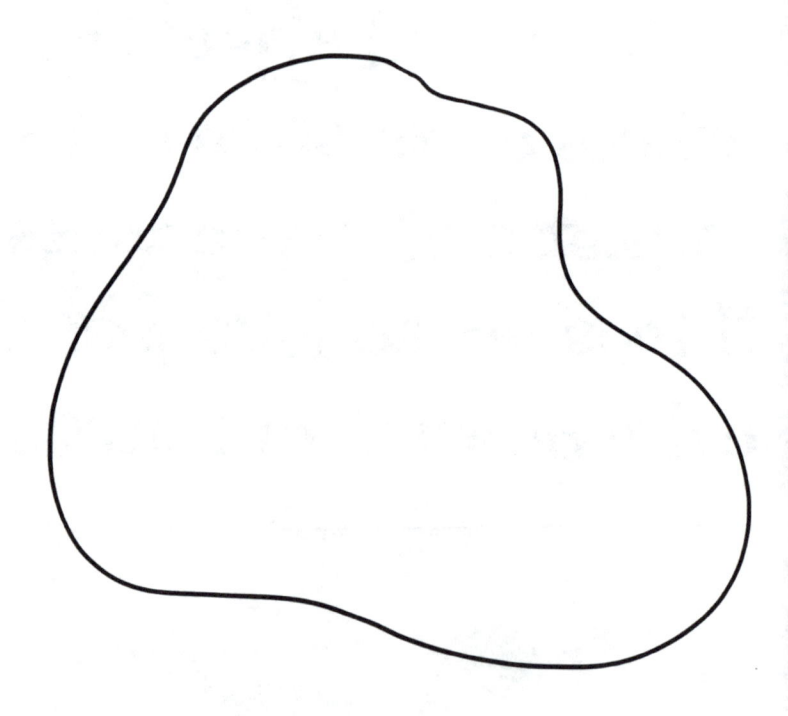

do's and don'ts
when someone you love comes out to you as aspec

don't say

"why didn't you realize this sooner?"

"what about (insert person's name here), didn't you like them?"

"you're too young to know for sure."

"I knew something was wrong with you!"

"does this mean i'm not going to get any grandkids from you?"

"you just have to wait for the right person."

"aren't you worried you're making a huge mistake?

do say

"I love you."

"how has that felt for you?"

"how can I best support you?"

"that sounds hard."

"I am spending time learning about this so that I can understand better."

"you matter to me."

"thank you for trusting me with this. I'll keep it in confidence for you."

talk to the person you love about what they need. everyone is different! something might be validating to one person and hurtful to another.

common misconceptions about people on the ace spectrum

asexual people don't like sex.

actually, some asexual people do enjoy sex! they just might not feel sexual attraction with the person they are having it with.

asexual people can't be in relationships.

they definitely can, if that is something they are wanting! some people discover their identity as aspec in the middle of their marriage and find ways to make it a fulfilling/comfortable relationship for both partners.

asexual people are anti-sex.

there are asexual people that feel repulsed by sex, but that feeling does not always extend to others. it's incredibly common to have sex-positive attitudes and be asexual.

asexual people don't have a sex drive.

libido is completely separate from sexual attraction. asexual people can have high, medium, low, or nonexistent sex drives. it just depends on the person.

asexuality is an illness.

the belief that asexuality is a mental or physical disorder is incredibly harmful to aspec individuals and has led to false diagnoses, misdiagnosed medication, and attempts at conversion. asexuality is not the result of a hormone deficiency, or a syndrome, or a physical or psychological ailment. we don't need to be treated or fixed.

asexuality is a lifestyle choice.

being asexual is not a choice! and it is not the same thing as being celibate.

part two: survey

these quotes are from a survey I created with over 400 anonymous individualized responses from aspec individuals.

reading them was both powerful and so heartbreaking.

there are so many of us out there and yet it is so easy to feel completely alone in our aspec identities.

this is a reminder that you aren't.

What is something you wish more people knew about folks on the aspectrum?

"That it's not a phase, and it's not immaturity. Not a late bloomer, and that aromanticism/asexuality exists and is absolutely valid :) Romantic/sexual relationships aren't "the highest" of a relationship you can get/achieve in life."

"That asexual people can still have sex and aromantic people can still be in relationships. Also that not everyone who is asexual is aromantic and vice versa."

"That we're all very different and do not all fit the stereotypes. Also that we belong in the queer community."

"There is no one aspectrum experience. Everyone has a completely unique experience."

"That aspec identities are complicated even for the people on the spectrum and don't just boil down to cut and dry easy answers."

"The aromantic spectrum and the asexual spectrum are two distinct things, you can be aromantic allosexual, asexual alloromantic, or asexual aromantic. Aromantic people are not emotionless."

"You don't need to understand us just respect us"

"I don't need to live my life the way you live yours. I don't need to want the things you want. I don't need to have the same motivations you have. Big shocker here for you: people are different. And that's okay. You don't have to understand, you don't even have to accept it, you just have to keep your mouth shut and not be an asshole."

"I wish they knew we aren't some weirdos. It's just the way we live and it's a normal thing. We don't have to be repaired or seek for help."

"You're not too young to know"

"That what I feel at the moment might change or be wrong because I'm trying to discover myself but still want people I'm close with to know how I feel."

"I wish more people knew how difficult it is mentally to explore being on the aspectrum. It's hard to gauge what is "normal" in terms of level of attraction and whether you have a lesser amount than "normal", and even harder if you're not exactly sure what attraction is supposed to feel like in the first place. Add in all the societal pressure on sex and relationships, and even if you get over feeling "broken", you might never get over the feeling that you're "missing" something."

"All aspec people are different. If a person doesn't want some kind of relationship, you shouldn't feel sorry for them, because it is probably ok for them not to have it. A person can be happy being single. And also the understanding of your own asexuality and aromanticism can take a lot of time. I mean, years! So there are people who discover that they are on the a-spectrum in their 30s, 40s or later and that's ok."

"We exist. We aren't "broken." We can face rejection, intrusive questioning, harassment, and possibly violence for being "out." If we're not ready to "come out," we can live with the fear or stress of being "outed." Other queer folx not understanding or believing us really hurts, because we need more people on our side. And we are an incredibly diverse and colorful group from a variety of backgrounds, places, and walks of life with varying experiences."

"We know ourselves. We don't need help."

"Lack of romantic attraction/feelings doesn't mean you don't form strong bonds with partners or that you care about them any less"

"We're not broken or missing something"

"That we exist. :)"

"That we exist"

"We exist"

part three: reflection

what has been most helpful to me in exploring/accepting myself in my identity?

_____

_____

_____

_____

_____

what has been most harmful to me in exploring/accepting myself in my identity?

what are some aspects of my identity that I feel very sure about?

_____

_____

_____

_____

_____

_____

_____

what are some parts that I am still figuring out?

what does it feel like to be in my body today?

_____

_____

_____

_____

_____

_____

_____

draw some people or things that make me feel safe and/or loved

graphical representations of me

(while keeping in mind that things can change and fluctuate, and that's okay)

if you need some extra help understanding the terms used:

bi- more than one gender attraction
pan- all gender attraction
hetero- other/opposite gender attraction
homo- same gender attraction
sex drive- libido

```
        BI/PAN
HETEROSEXUAL   HOMOSEXUAL



         ASEXUAL
```

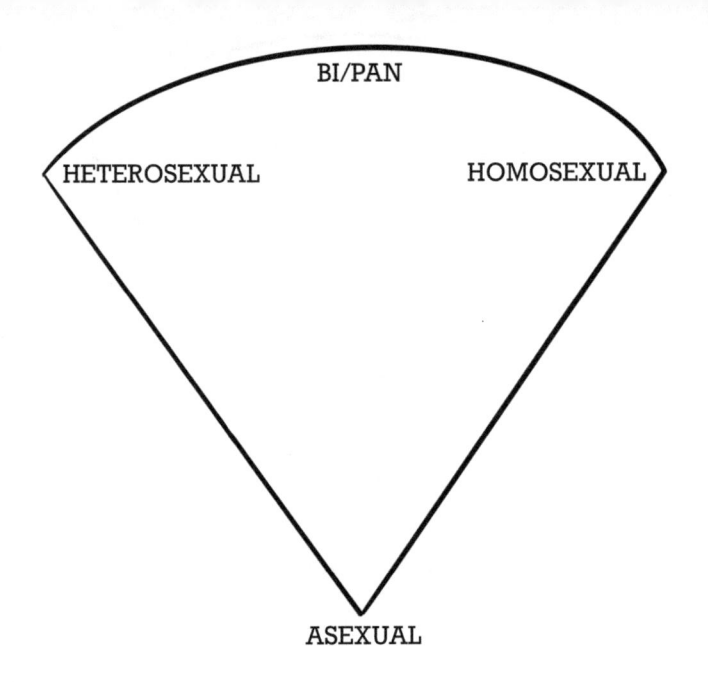

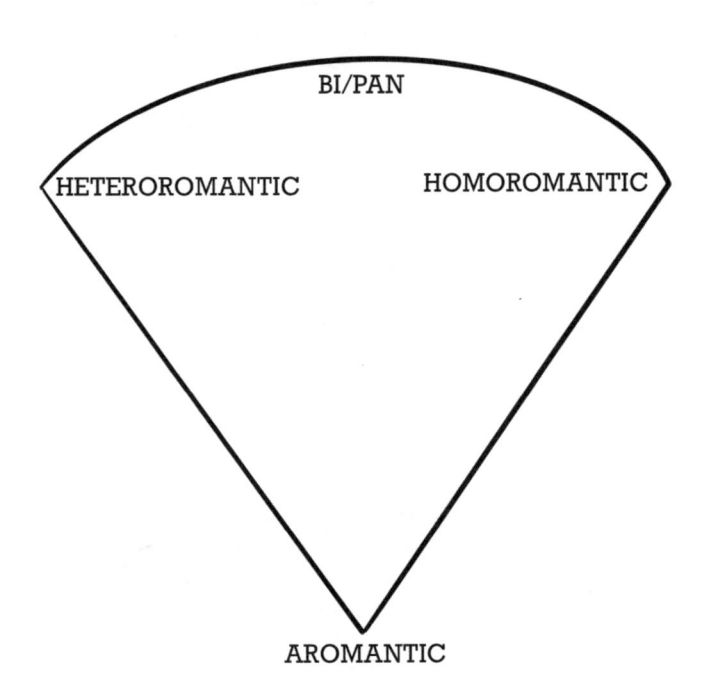

```
         BI/PAN
HETEROROMANTIC   HOMOROMANTIC



        AROMANTIC
```

BI/PAN

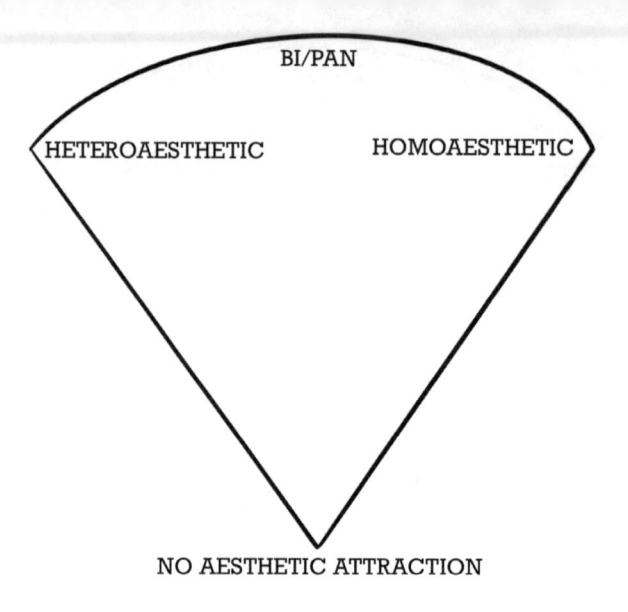

HETEROAESTHETIC   HOMOAESTHETIC

NO AESTHETIC ATTRACTION

sex

repulsed   indifferent   favorable

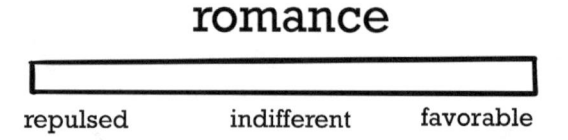

romance

repulsed   indifferent   favorable

sex drive

none/low   moderate   high

# part four: identities index

ace spectrum
identities index

Aceflux- Someone whose sexual orientation fluctuates but generally stays on the asexual spectrum

Acespike- An identity where an individual is typically asexual but occasionally experiences short, sudden bursts of sexual attraction

Acevague- When your identity as ace is partially or fully influenced by neurodivergence

Aegosexual- A disconnect between oneself and the subject of sexual arousal

Akoisexual- A person who experiences sexual attraction but their feelings fade or disappear if reciprocated

Apothisexual- Someone under the asexual umbrella who is sex repulsed

Apresexual- An identity where sexual attraction is only felt after another type of attraction is formed

Aroace- Someone who identifies as both aromantic and asexual

Asexual- The lack of sexual attraction to other people, experiencing little to no sexual attraction

Caedsexual- Someone who feels they were at one point allosexual, but that it was taken away from past trauma

Cupiosexual- A label for those who do not experience sexual attraction but still desire or like sexual relationships

Demisexual- Only feeling sexual attraction when a strong emotional bond has been formed first

Fictosexual- Anyone who experiences exclusive sexual attraction toward fictional characters

Fraysexual- When someone experiences sexual attraction but loses it as they get to know a person

Graysexual- People who experience limited sexual attraction, whether that is rarely or with low intensity

Lithsexual- A person who only feels sexual attraction when it is not reciprocated or acted upon

Novisexual- When a person feels that their sexual attraction is too complicated to attach to a label

Placiosexual- Someone who enjoys performing sexual acts for other people but does not want them reciprocated

Reciprosexual- A person who does not feel sexual attraction unless they know another person is sexually attracted to them first

Requiesexual- Having limited to no sexual attraction due to some form of emotional exhaustion

Quoisexual- Not knowing where one fits on the spectrum or not identifying with any existing label

Did I forget any? Write them down here!

_____

_____

_____

_____

_____

_____

_____

part five: resources

Websites and Communities:

Asexual Visibility and Education Network (AVEN)

Ace Week website and event

Asexual and Aromantic subreddit pages

AUREA website

Books with Aspec Characters:

Loveless by Alice Oseman

Every Heart a Doorway by Seanan McGuire

Let's Talk About Love by Claire Kann

How to Be a Normal Person by T.J. Klune

Books on Asexuality:

The Invisible Orientation by Julie Sondra Decker

Understanding Asexuality by Anthony Bogaert

Asexuality: A Brief Introduction by Asexuality Archive

Ace: What Asexuality Reveals About Desire, Society, and the Meaning of Sex by Angela Chen

Support:

LGBT National Youth Hotline (800-246-7743)

LGBT National Hotline (888-843-4564)

You are not alone. Feel free to reach out to me through social media. My dms are always open! instagram: alittlebookoface

author's note

Hi, I'm Clara. I am six feet tall and like rain and nachos and socks with art on them. I also happen to be asexual and aromantic. I decided to write this illustrated book as a way to explain, educate, and share about the different experiences of people in asexual and aromantic (aspec) communities. When I first came out, I really wanted to have a book to be able to share with my friends and family- and myself- that explained what these identities meant to me and others.

Unfortunately, there weren't a lot of options. So I decided to write my own! It definitely isn't perfect, but I have spent hours researching and gathering data through surveys to try to include everyone's different aspec experiences in this book.

Because one very important thing to know about being on the ace and/or aro spectrums is that it means something different for everyone. And that's okay! All stories are valid and important!

One thing that I have learned as of late is that educating yourself is a great way to make the world a little bit safer for marginalized communities.

Even if something is initially hard to understand, opening your mind to the fact that other people experience the world differently than you is an important and valuable thing to do.

I hope that you are able to find value in this book, whether you are hoping to show up better for someone who you love, explore your own identity, learn something new, or anything in between.

all the best,
clara

my notes:

Made in United States
Cleveland, OH
28 July 2025